NATIONAL GEOGRAPHIC

D0503545

Watching
Chimps

PATHFINDER EDITION

By Peter Winkler

CONTENTS

Hanging Out With Chimps

BY PETER WINKLER

These African apes are smart, social—and always surprising.

"**W**here's Jane?" No one knew. Four-year-old Jane Goodall had vanished. Her mother searched the English countryside for hours, but she had no luck. It was time to call the police.

Then someone came running. Yes, it was Jane, but she smelled awful, she had straw all over her clothes, and she was smiling.

Jane had been inside a chicken coop. Why? Well, she wanted to see how a hen lays eggs, so she sat for hours—waiting and watching.

Jane's mother didn't get mad. Instead, she listened and supported Jane's curiosity. That encouragement sparked a great career.

FROM CHICKENS TO CHIMPS

As Jane Goodall grew, so did her passion for nature. She saved up and went to Africa, where she met Louis Leakey, a famous scientist.

In 1960, Leakey sent Goodall to a place called Gombe (GAHM bee). It is a wildlife reserve in the country of Tanzania (tan zuh NEE uh). Her job was to study chimpanzees, a type of **ape**. At first the apes ran off anytime they saw Goodall, but, after a while, they got used to her.

Goodall watched eagerly—hour after hour, day after day, and she took careful notes. Her work gave the world a new picture of chimps.

AT WORK IN THE WILD

Understanding chimps is a huge task, so Goodall created the Gombe Stream Research Centre in 1965 so others could help.

Gombe researchers eat breakfast before dawn, and then they trek into the woods. Meanwhile, the chimps are asleep—high in the trees. They will wake up at first light, so researchers need to be nearby.

Dream Job. *As a girl, Jane Goodall (near left) loved animals. As an adult, she studied African chimpanzees (far left).*

What happens next? Well, that's up to the chimpanzees. Researchers usually follow an individual or a small group. One scientist, for instance, studies how chimps care for their young, so she focuses on a mom and kids.

FOLLOW THAT CHIMP!

Keeping up with chimpanzees is a challenge, but fortunately, they take plenty of breaks. Chimps pause to eat, play, nap, and enjoy being together. Like humans, they're truly social animals.

Chimps spend a lot of time **grooming**— carefully searching through each other's hair, they pick out any dirt or pests. Grooming relaxes chimpanzees, and it strengthens their friendships, too.

Sunset is bedtime, and up in the trees, chimps make nests out of branches and leaves. Soon they fall asleep, so that's when the researchers trudge home. Another wild day is over.

Not Too Close! *At first Jane Goodall touched and groomed wild chimps, but now she keeps her distance. Why? Scientists have learned that chimps can catch diseases from humans.*

EXTREME SCIENCE PROJECT

Like all scientists, Gombe researchers collect **data**, or facts. Some carry checklists of chimpanzee actions. At set times, each chimp-watcher notes what an ape is doing.

Each night the researchers create a map that shows where people saw chimps that day.

Researchers also use cameras, video recorders, and other high-tech tools. Yet the heart of the job remains simple: You watch chimps, you write about chimps, and you think about chimps.

All those checklists, maps, notes, photos, and videos add up to a mound of information. Observing chimps at Gombe has become one of the most important animal studies ever.

BIG DISCOVERY

Jane Goodall got a huge surprise her very first year at Gombe. She watched chimps "fish" for termites. The chimps gently poked twigs and grass stems into a termite nest. Sometimes they stripped leaves from the twigs. In other words, the chimps made and used tools!

That was major news. Humans had believed that only people made tools.

KARL AMMANN, CORBIS

Some scientists refused to believe Goodall until she photographed the apes in action.

Chimps use other tools as well. To get water from hollows in branches or logs, they make "sponges" by scrunching up leaves. In some places, chimps use rocks to crack open nuts.

SOUND FAMILIAR?

Chimpanzees are intelligent, and they can be tender, but they can also be brutal. Does that remind you of any other **species**? Yes, chimps and humans are alike in some amazing ways.

Most chimpanzee mothers are protective, affectionate, and playful. So are chimp older brothers and sisters because they help care for the babies. Sometimes chimps even "adopt" orphans.

But chimps are not always appealing. In the 1970s, a deadly war broke out between chimp groups, and one group got totally wiped out. Also, chimp mothers sometimes kill and eat others' babies.

"When I first started at Gombe," Goodall said, "I thought the chimps were nicer than we are, but time has revealed that they are not." Like humans, chimpanzees are good, bad, and complicated.

Tooling Around. *Termites are tasty snacks that chimps like to eat. To catch them, chimps make tools by turning branches into "fishing rods." Learning that chimps make tools was probably Jane Goodall's biggest discovery.*

TOMORROW AT GOMBE

Gombe Stream Research Centre began as one woman with guts and binoculars, but now it includes dedicated researchers and visiting scientists. Before sunrise tomorrow, they'll head back into the forest for more chimp-watching.

Jane Goodall probably won't join them because since 1985, she's spent most of her time traveling. She tells people around the world about chimpanzees—and how important it is to save them.

Wordwise

ape: bonobo, chimpanzee, gibbon, gorilla, orangutan, or siamang

data: facts

groom: to clean another chimp's hair and skin with the fingers

species: type of living thing

Chimp Ranges

MOROCCO
TUNISIA
Mediterranean Sea
ALGERIA
LIBYA
EGYPT
WESTERN SAHARA
Morocco
N
W E
S
Red Sea
30
MAURITANIA
MALI
NIGER
CHAD
SUDAN
ERITREA
DJIBOUT
20
SENEGAL
GAMBIA
GUINEA
BURKINA FASO
BENIN
GHANA
NIGERIA
CENTRAL AFRICAN REPUBLIC
ETHIOPIA
10°N
CÔTE D'IVOIRE
CAMEROON
GUINEA-BISSAU
LIBERIA
TOGO
EQUATORIAL GUINEA
GABON
CONGO
DEMOCRATIC REPUBLIC OF CONGO
UGANDA
KENYA
SOMALIA
0°
SIERRA LEONE
Atlantic Ocean
SAO TOME & PRINCIPE
Angola
BURUNDI
Gombe National Park
RWANDA
TANZANIA
India Ocea
SEYCHELL
10°S
COMORO
ANGOLA
MALAWI
ZAMBIA
MOZAMBIQUE
MADAGASCA
ZIMBABWE
NAMIBIA
BOTSWANA
SWAZILAND
SOUTH AFRICA
LESOTHO
30

Where chimpanzees lived in the wild 100 years ago

Where chimpanzees live in the wild today

0   1,000 miles
0   1,000 kilometers
Lambert Azimuthal Equal-Area projection

Two million chimpanzees lived in Africa a century ago, and their range, or territory, stretched for thousands of miles along the Equator.

Today there are perhaps only 150,000 chimps, and they are in danger because they face the threat of extinction, or dying out.

What happened? Africa's human population grew, and people needed more land, so they chopped down forests. That left countless chimps without homes.

Humans also kill chimps—often illegally. "Bush meat" from wild animals earns a lot of money.

Can we save chimpanzees? It won't be easy. People will need to find better ways to treat Earth.

But Jane Goodall has hope: "We can change the world."

Tools for Chimp-Watchers

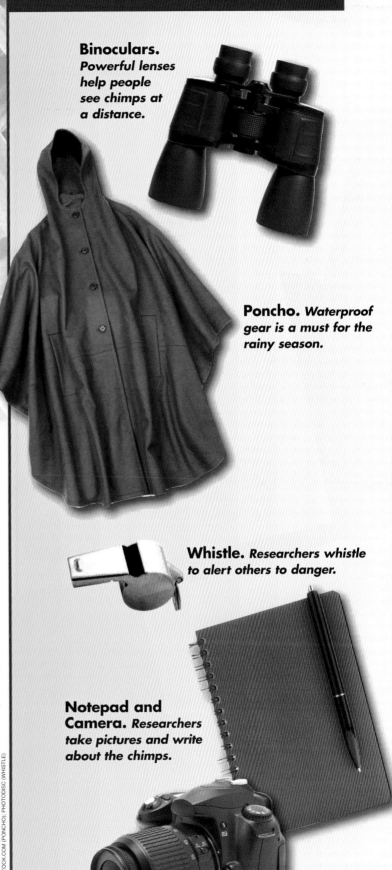

Binoculars. *Powerful lenses help people see chimps at a distance.*

Poncho. *Waterproof gear is a must for the rainy season.*

Whistle. *Researchers whistle to alert others to danger.*

Notepad and Camera. *Researchers take pictures and write about the chimps.*

Wild About

Baby Care

Charging Displays

Each Other

Chimp moms spend a lot of time cuddling their babies. Young chimps also get a lot of attention from brothers, sisters, and other members of their extended family.

Chimps are social animals, which means they like to hang out with other chimps. They're similar to people in that way. Chimp babies spend most of their time snuggling with their moms, while brother and sister chimps play with each other in the woods.

With all that time together, chimps do a lot of talking. They don't speak, but they do make sounds to show how they feel. They scream, grunt, pant, hoot, squeak, or roar. Each sound says something slightly different.

Chimps can speak volumes with their faces, too. Like people, they express themselves as they grin, pout, or purse their lips. Their expressions change with their moods, so a chimp's face tells how the animal feels. A chimp has many expressions that show others how it is feeling.

Chimps also use gestures to get a point across. A chimp may wave its hand to get another chimp to follow. Sometimes chimps throw tantrums. They throw their bodies around and holler. But chimps can also show a softer side. They tease or tickle and take time out to play. How else do chimps communicate? What do their behaviors say?

To look tough, male chimps can put on quite a show. They run around, stamp their feet, throw things, and make lots of noise.

Greeting Gestures

Chimps touch a lot. That's especially true after being apart. They say "hello" with hugs, grunts, pats, and kisses.

Observing

Scientists learn about chimps by observing them. What does observing really mean? It means watching carefully. Scientists pay close attention to the sounds chimps make. They watch how the animals move and how other chimps react.

Part of observing is asking questions. One scientist may want to find out how a mother cares for her young. Another might want to know if chimps have leaders. These scientists will observe, or watch for, different things.

As scientists observe, they also take notes. They jot down what they see and hear, so observing isn't quite the same as looking. When you look at something, your eyes see it. When you observe, your mind takes a much closer look.

You don't have to go to a faraway place to observe animals. You can study a pet. Start by picking a favorite pet. It can be your own or a friend's. Then use the activity on page 11 to learn about the animal.

Animals

✎ Observe a pet every day for a week.

✎ Take notes about what you see.

✎ When you are finished, use your notes to draw conclusions about the pet and its behavior.

Animal Name: Muffin

Type of Animal: Cat

My question: How much time do cats spend grooming?

Day 1: Muffin licked fur for 10 minutes before bed.

Day 2: I saw Muffin grooming her face for 3 minutes after eating this morning.

Day 3: Muffin groomed before taking a nap, and again when she woke up.

My conclusion: Cats spend a lot of time licking themselves clean.

How I know: Every day, Muffin cleaned herself after eating, before sleeping, and when she woke up.

Other questions I have: How much time do cats spend asleep versus awake?

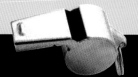

Chimpanzees

It's time to find out what you learned about chimp research.

1 How was Jane Goodall's childhood important to her career as a scientist?

2 Why do scientists say that chimps are social animals?

3 What is the most important tool used by Gombe researchers? Why?

4 Why do people say that chimps are good, bad, and complicated?

5 How do chimps communicate?